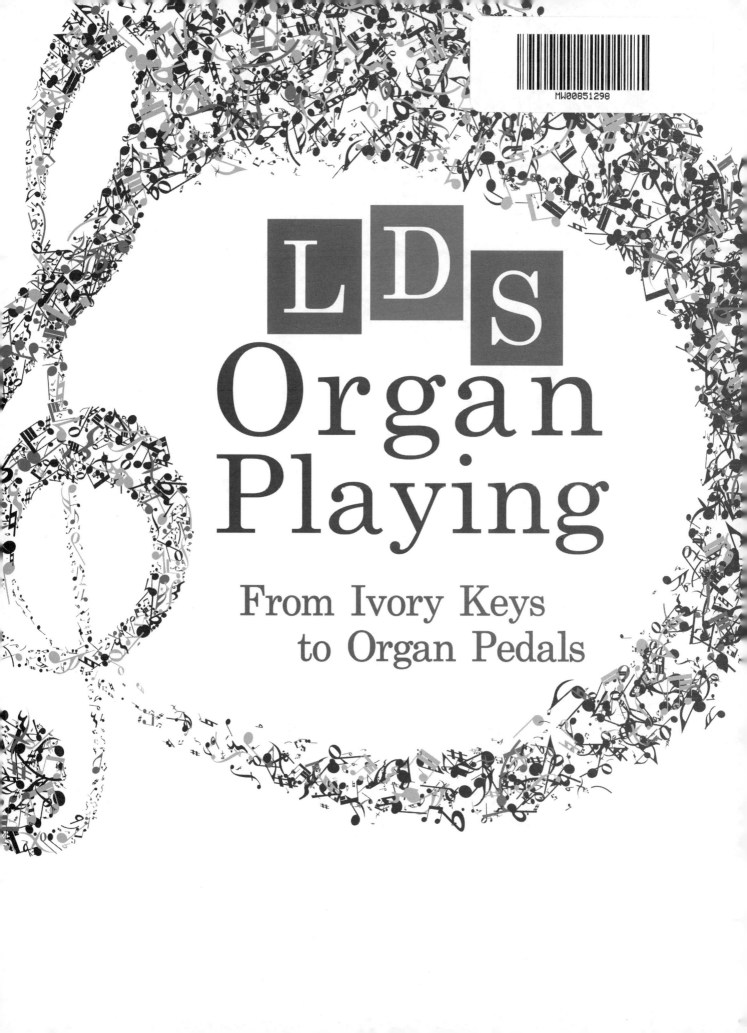

LDS

Organ Playing

From Ivory Keys to Organ Pedals

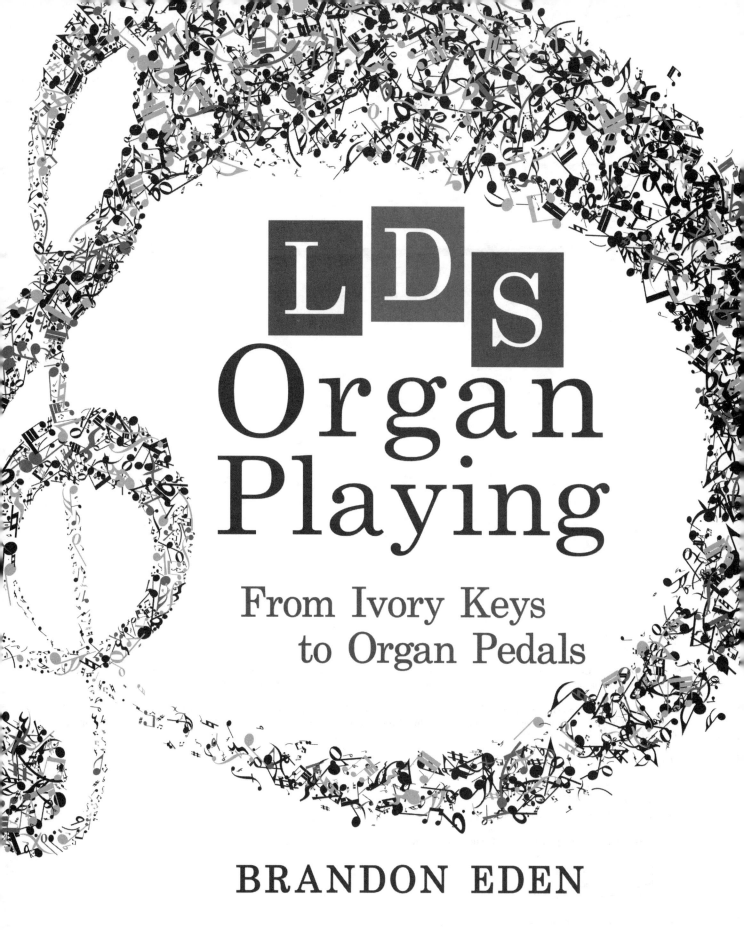

LDS Organ Playing

From Ivory Keys to Organ Pedals

BRANDON EDEN

CFI
An Imprint of Cedar Fort, Inc.
Springville, Utah

© 2016 Brandon Eden

This is not an official publication of The Church of Jesus Christ of Latter-day Saints. The opinions and views expressed herein belong solely to the author and do not necessarily represent the opinions or views of Cedar Fort, Inc. Permission for the use of sources, graphics, and photos is also solely the responsibility of the author.

ISBN 13: 978-1-4621-1847-2

Published by CFI, an imprint of Cedar Fort, Inc.
2373 W. 700 S., Springville, UT 84663
Distributed by Cedar Fort, Inc., www.cedarfort.com

LIBRARY OF CONGRESS CONTROL NUMBER: 2016936064

Cover design by Shawnda T. Craig
Cover design © 2016 Cedar Fort, Inc.
Edited and typeset by Kevin Haws

Printed in the United States of America

10 9 8 7 6 5 4 3 2 1

Printed on acid-free paper

For Katie, Sammie, and CJ—my inspiration

Contents

Introduction

I t's the second Sunday in a new ward, and we've officially announced that we're staying for the long haul. Now we're sitting relatively comfortably in the bishop's office, awaiting our obligatory "getting-to-know-you" interview. After the standard introductory phrases and wheres and whys, he asks the inevitable question: "So, Brother Eden, what do you do outside of work?"

"Well, I play the piano."

The reaction that follows is one of two. First, a short but pronounced semi-awkward silence before the discussion shifts to my wife. Second, just shy of the hallelujah chorus ringing through the halls.

Regardless of the reaction, the end result stays the same. Next week, I return to the bishop's office, where I learn that, after much deliberation, the bishopric would like to extend me a calling: the ward organist.

"You do realize that the organ and piano are two completely different instruments, right? You can't just ride a motorcycle once you know how to drive a car, can you?" At least that's what I would like to say. What I *do* is nod my head and grit my teeth, and in no time I'm sitting in front of the entire congregation and stumbling my way through some semblance of "O Savior, Thou Who Wearest a Crown" because the chorister assumes I can play anything due to my extensive training.

This has happened to me in basically every new ward I've moved into since graduating high school (seven and counting now). Thankfully, the transition for me hasn't been too terrible. I actually enjoy playing the organ—extremely loud volumes are my thing. After over ten years of looking for subs but finding people who "only play the piano" or trying to remove myself from having multiple simultaneous callings (organist, Primary pianist, choir pianist, stake organist, and so on). I have decided to put together a guide of sorts to help pianists transition to the fear-inspiring organ.

Similarities between the Organ and the Piano

Before I get too far in, I want to define what I mean by a trained pianist. Sitting at a piano while some silver-haired lady looks over your shoulder is what usually comes to mind. But I am mainly referring to someone who can read music with solid efficiency and has a strong foundation in music theory. I am not spending any time on the basics of music or keyboard playing.

Introduction

Even though they look fairly similar to the untrained eye, the piano and organ have little in common. Basically, only the arrangement and the size of the keys are the same. So don't feel bad if the organ is imposing to you. The good news is that your fingers do instinctively know where to go. Chords and octaves are the same size and layout on the organ as they are on the piano, so you don't have to relearn muscle memory.

Well, at least not too much.

Differences between the Organ and the Piano

Most organs throughout the Church are not the typical pipe organ. They are electronic and use a fancy computer to make all the little doohickeys work. I, however, am going to talk as if you are on a pipe organ, because most electronic organs do try to mimic how a pipe organ behaves.

1. There are too many keyboards! What do I do with the extra keyboards?

The multiple keyboards (called *manuals* in organ-speak), plus an even more daunting set of pedals, cause most pianists to duck their heads in the sand. Because the two-keyboard setup is by far the most common configuration in chapels, I'm going to assume that is what you will be using. The top keyboard is called the *Swell* and the bottom is called the *Great*.

2. Where is Middle C?

The exact middle of a regular piano is technically E and F, while Middle C is below them. The organ follows a similar procedure. The exact middle, in this case, is F and G, while Middle C is the one below them. So yes, you don't have nearly as many bass or treble notes. But, as you will see later, you won't need them.

3. So which keyboard do I use?

Technically, it doesn't matter. The *Great* is located, in relation to the bench, closer to where the keyboard on a piano would be, so I usually play there. Because the *Great* is the main manual, it usually has access to bolder sounds. I use the *Swell* for softer sounds.

4. Is it normal to feel like I'm falling off the bench?

As pianists, we're trained to sit at the edge of the piano bench so we can use our legs to help stabilize us while we play. That is not the case on the organ. You need to sit all the way back on the bench, just like you do at a picnic table. You'll most likely be pulling the bench closer to the keys than you would a piano bench, and your feet should dangle or rest lightly on the pedals.

Also, you shouldn't be putting any excessive weight on your feet. Yes, that means take off your shoes! Unless your shoes are designed for the organ (thin and light), they will get in the way and just add dead weight to your legs. My clod hoppers make my legs go to sleep if I keep them on.

5. I know these switches are called stops, but what are they?

This is where most of the fun comes from playing the organ. These stops are the different sounds that the organ makes. A quick history lesson on the name: Originally, organs were connected to a large number of pipes. This is still true in the Tabernacle and the Conference Center but is becoming more and more rare in chapels. (Organs cost a ton to maintain.) These pipes function just like a whistle. You blow air through them and they make a note. Back in the good old days, two less-than-happy people—choirboys, usually—would actually have to pump the air manually. Now a machine does the pumping. An organ really only needs one set of pipes to work, but that got boring really fast. So they started making more and more different types, or ranks. They would be various lengths, thickness, and shapes, and all would make a different sound. If an organist wants to "stop" a certain row rank of pipes, he or she pushes in the stop—hence the name. On real pipe organs, a physical piece would actually slide into place and prevent air from flowing through the pipe.

As a side note, this is where we get the phrase *pull out all the stops*. When you do that on an organ, every rank is activated, and things get really loud really fast. For your purposes, they're just different sounds. I recommend playing them to see what you like. Many are named after different instruments because they sound vaguely similar. You should have one set of stops for each manual, or keyboard.

6. *Why don't some of the stops work?*

Many ranks of pipes only really have one volume—loud—so they won't activate until the volume is turned up. Also, some electronic organs have presets that can't be changed. A preset is a previous setting that was recorded into the organ. Check to see if you're able to change presets by referring to the organ manual (a copy should be in your Church library).

7. *So what are all these buttons?*

This is where the exact model of organ comes into play, and because I don't know which one you have, you'll need to refer to the manual for specifics. The most common buttons are for presets. Imagine that you are playing "Praise to the Man," and you want the final verse to be bigger and bolder than the previous three. You could try your hand at quick draw and pull ten different stops in the one-second gap between verses, or you can easily push one of the buttons located conveniently below where your fingers play. A quick press of the thumb, and your entire setup can change. There is even a row above the pedals.

This, of course, does take some advanced planning—but not too much. Basically, you would set the stops the way you like and press and hold one of the buttons (just like setting the radio station in your car). Many organs have a separate "set" or "setting" button that you have to hold as well to program your preset. This type helps prevent you, or any curious child, from changing your presets accidently. When you press the numbered preset button in the future (don't press and hold this time), that exact setup you created previously will be selected.

One tip if you share the organ with another ward is to put a small strip of sticky tape next to a group of buttons with your ward name and do the same for all other wards with the other button groups. Most people get the hint and leave your buttons alone. This way, you can have your favorite four or five presets always ready. I have four myself. One is for loud, bold selections (like "The Star-Spangled Banner"), another is for normal but robust songs (like "We Thank Thee, O God, for a Prophet"), another is for milder songs (like "I Stand All Amazed"), and the last is for sacrament hymns.

There are many other buttons, and some of them will be covered later. Some won't be covered at all and can be specific to your organ.

8. *What does* Tutti *mean?*

It's an orchestral term meaning "all." Basically, it's a single button that opens all the stops. Use with caution. It can get loud *fast*. Pressing it a second time should send you back to where you started, though.

9. *There are a lot of other buttons that weren't mentioned. MIDI? Tremulant? What?*

I could go into detail as to what these do, but it doesn't really matter. They are so rarely used that you don't need to burden yourself (think *sostenuto* pedal). If you're dying to know, turn to the manual.

10. *What are those three gas pedals?*

I was asked this once by a fellow pianist and didn't know what he was talking about at first. I had him show me and was directed to the three-foot controllers just above the pedals. They kind of act like the gas pedal in your car, and the analogy actually stuck with me. These are the volume controllers, and they can mean different things on different organs. There are usually three of them—one for the overall volume (usually on the right) and one each for the manuals. (There is rarely a volume control for the pedals.) And just like the accelerator in the car, when the top tilts forward, the volume goes up.

Introduction

This actually leads to one of the most bizarre experiences for a pianist on the organ. The piano was originally called the pianoforte, meaning it could play loud and soft notes at the same time. Most of us are able to play three or four volumes at the same time, even in the same chord, if need be. We pianists pride ourselves in being able to do this type of voicing. But none of that is possible on the organ. It doesn't matter one iota how hard you push the keys down. It will not play any louder without adjusting the volume pedal. I always set the volume before I play and never touch it again until I'm getting ready for the next song.

11. Well, that's annoying. How do I make the melody stand out?

Basically, you don't. You can select different ranks of pipes that accentuate higher pitch like a flute, but that's about it.

12. Will that present a problem for the congregation?

No. They won't notice, and most likely you didn't either before now. But it does bring up a lesser-known factoid about how volume works on an organ. On a piano, there's only one way to make the note louder: strike harder. One an organ, there are three ways. The most obvious is to send more air through the pipes. More air equals more volume, just like singing. Another way is to add a rank of pipes. This makes sense, but you need to realize that this isn't a gradual increase in volume. Add a rank of pipes, and in one instant, it is louder and sounds a little different. No subtlety there. The last method involves using organ doors. Real pipes are built into a box of some kind (except the massive ones like in the Tabernacle or Conference Center). This box has a front made of a series of wooden slats—like a sideways venetian curtain—that can be physically moved to open up the box to the congregation. As you might imagine, the sound would be muffled before the box is open. Once it's open, the volume change is fairly linear until the slats are perpendicular to the pipes.

13. Thanks for the history lesson, but I don't have a real pipe organ. What does this mean for an electronic organ?

Most electronic organs do what they can to emulate real organs. Basically, what you need to get out of this is that the volume controllers don't necessarily behave the same way the volume dial on your radio does. The volume jumps instead of glides. It's best to set the volume for one entire song and not worry about changing it.

14. Okay. I get it now, but it still feels funny to play. What's going on?

This is the second major performance difference between an organ and a piano. The feel of the keyboard is not only caused by the material of the key, but also by the moving parts involved. This entire setup is called the *Action*. A single note in a piano can have as many as forty moving parts, which feels a whole lot different than the standard two in an organ. Sadly, you'll just have to get used to this. It isn't too hard, but because volume isn't controlled by the keys, you can't accidently hit a note louder than the surrounding ones.

15. Where is the damper?

This is another seemingly small thing that creates tons of frustration in pianists. There's no way to sustain any of the notes without simply holding the note down. This is even more difficult to deal with because the sound instantly disappears when you remove your finger. This can make playing *legato* rather difficult.

There are a few ways to deal with this problem. The most straightforward method is to practice your *legato* training from back in the day. I remember hours at the piano spent being forbidden from using the damper while still not leaving gaps between notes.

This is also where a nifty little cheat can come in handy. As most of you are aware, the music in the hymnal is neither organ music nor piano music; it's choral music. It's written for four groups of people to sing. And it's abnormal for every single part to change notes between chordings. That means usually one of the parts holds the same note for two or more note groupings. You can easily hold that note through all of those groupings. Here are some examples.

Example 1

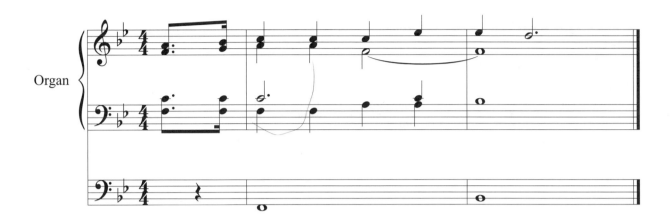

Organ

Example 2

Organ

The congregation will never know, and it'll sound smooth. Using the pedals can also alleviate some of the *legato* problems.

16. Ah yes, the pedals. What do I do with those?

This is the number one reason that people give me as an excuse for not playing the organ. And it's understandable on a certain level. Most pianists I know are rather nitpicky about playing their instrument (let's face it: they're perfectionists) and don't like missing notes or worse, playing that infamous "jazz note." So the transition from one stationary foot and one that moves slightly up and down to *two* moving feet is scary at best—terrifying for most people.

And to top it off, that note isn't even written down. Great! Now I have to extrapolate the chord (inversion of said chord) and, without looking, move my foot laterally and play a note all on the fly? I don't think so!

Using the pedals is pretty daunting at first glance. But the obvious solution is to not play the pedals. Thus far, I have never heard of people complaining about organists not playing the pedals. And if they did, I would suggest that perhaps *they* should be the one playing. That would nip the complaint in the bud right away.

17. Does organ music have to sound weak and thin? (Even if no one says anything, everyone is thinking it!)

While I personally believe that most people don't care, one of the joys of playing the organ is the power. Much of that power is supplied by the pedals. So I have a nifty little fix for you. Every organ has a cheat built in, but it can have different names, so I will describe it generally. Somewhere on the organ is a switch or button that slaves the bass pedals to the *Great* manual.

Excuse the techno babble—I will explain in more detail.

Once this function is engaged, the computer inside the organ looks for the lowest note played on the *Great* manual below middle C. It then plays the corresponding pedal for you. The physical pedal won't move, but it will play as if you had just stepped on it. Here are some examples to diagram what is happening.

When you play this . . .

Example 3a

. . . then this sounds.

Example 3b

When you play this . . .

Example 4a

. . . then this sounds.

Example 4b

It's magic! I've just solved almost all of the problems associated with one wonderful little button. The hardest part is finding it, and you may have to look in the instruction manual or try it out with some trial and error on the buttons. The most common name I have seen is "Pedal Coupler." But I've also seen "Bass," "Octaver," "Pedal to *Great*," and so on. I use this all of the time, basically whenever I'm feeling lazy, or the song looks really hard. I even get compliments from real organ players at how adept I am at my pedal work. I usually then just smile and nod.

A word of caution when you decide to rely on this method: If you lift the bottom note while holding higher notes still below middle C (by accident or not), one of two things will happen. Either the bass will disappear completely or it will get "reassigned" to the new bottom note. It depends on your organ. Test it out to see what happens and make note for future reference. It's a weird quirk, but workable. It's usually good to try to hold the bottom note until it changes, instead of repeatedly hitting it like the following example.

Example 5

18. That's pretty nifty, but if I would like to try the pedals, where do I begin?

I have always felt that challenges make life interesting, and this is a more pleasurable one. If things get too difficult, I just press the magic button and stop worrying about it. But when I do want to play the pedals, I have a relatively simple process to do so.

Follow the bass notes. Many hymns are relatively simple, and you can sight-read the bass notes. "Sweet Hour of Prayer," for instance, only uses three bass notes, and they don't change often. It isn't too difficult to simply follow those changes. You shouldn't press the bass note every time, though. Just press and hold until the next change. Much more often, it sounds awkward from the excessive pumping. This is actually how the organ is intended to be played. But many of the hymns have an elaborate bass line and can be too overwhelming. In this case, I follow these next rules.

Follow the chords. This one might take a little prep work, but not too much. "A Poor Wayfaring Man of Grief," for example, only has two chords in the entire song, even though the hands play many different bass notes. You can easily put both feet into position and switch when necessary. For these songs, I just mark a big letter above each chord change beforehand. It takes about three minutes, and I'm golden.

Write it out. I actually try to avoid this step and just press the magic button. But if I'm feeling overly ambitious, which usually means I really like the song, I will write out the full bass line. I happen to have notation software, but there's no problem with penciling in the bass progression. Either do it really lightly or get your own hymnal. I usually follow a combination of the bass notes, chord progressions, and leading tones when moving my feet. It's a little too complicated for me to do on the fly, so I need it written down. The good news is that there really is no right or wrong way to do this so long as it sounds good.

19. I think I'm getting the hang of it. Do you have any little secrets?

The only "secret" I have is to not worry too much. If you, a picky perfectionist, are sitting in the congregation, and the organist plays a wrong note, you don't care. You're just grateful someone is doing it. That is how everyone else feels as well (if they even notice the wrong note).

20. Yes, yes, yes. I understand, but do you have any real secrets?

Set things up beforehand. I get to church thirty minutes early and prep. I've been doing this so long that just about every hymn is edited for my purposes, but I still like to make sure that each preset is how I want it.

21. I am fairly comfortable on the organ now. Is there anything I can do to spice it up?

On the concept of improvisation, or varying in any way from the actual written notes, the general consensus is . . . there really isn't a general consensus. Basically, if the bishop doesn't have a problem with it, then there isn't a problem. If he does, then it's probably in your best interest to just follow the notes.

In the sheet music section immediately following this, I have ten hymns written out. Each hymn has two versions. The first is the exact same as in the hymnal, with the pedal notes written out. I know when I first started, I had trouble deciding which note I should play, and this helped immensely. The second version is what I classify as acceptable deviation. These are simple variations on the hymnal version to add a little spice to a performance and—as of yet—have not offended anyone. You, of course, can create any sort of variation you please, but remember that the organ is meant as accompaniment to the singing, not a time for demonstrating your skill. I have been present when an organist did tons of embellishments and chord changes and even did a key change on the last verse. The congregation nearly stopped singing, not because they were awed by the beautiful music, but because they were lost and left behind. The song was "Praise to the Man." Imagine how crazy things must have become if a Church congregation in Utah couldn't figure out where they were while singing "Praise to the Man."

While I am accompanying the congregation, I use the embellished version for the short introduction and the normal version for all the initial verses. If I'm feeling comfortable, I use the embellished version for the final verse. I find that this helps give a sense of finality and give me a sense of pleasure that I'm magnifying my calling. For your convenience, in the following hymns, I have included the time duration of playing one verse at the top right of the sheet music. This should help you pick out a prelude song that will end just as the conductor steps up to the podium.

A Poor Wayfaring Man of Grief

music by George Coles
arranged by Brandon Eden
0:55

A Poor Wayfaring Man of Grief Variation

music by George Coles
arranged by Brandon Eden

0:55

Come, Come, Ye Saints

arranged by Brandon Eden

0:39

With Conviction ♩ = 80

Organ

Come, Come, Ye Saints Variation

arranged by Brandon Eden

0:39

With Conviction ♩ = 80

Have I Done Any Good?

music by Will L Thompson
arranged by Brandon Eden

0:54

14

Have I Done Any Good? Variation

music by Will L Thompson
arranged by Brandon Eden

0:54

17

High on the Mountain Top

music by Ebenezer Beesley
arranged by Brandon Eden

0:29

High on the Mountain Top Variation

music by Ebenezer Beesley
arranged by Brandon Eden

0:29

I Know That My Redeemer Lives

music by Lewis D Edwards
arranged by Brandon Eden

0:51

I Know That My Redeemer Lives Variation

music by Lewis D Edwards
arranged by Brandon Eden

0:51

Joseph Smith's First Prayer

music by Sylvanus B Pond
arranged by Brandon Eden
0:45

Joseph Smith's First Prayer Variation

music by Sylvanus B Pond
arranged by Brandon Eden
0:45

Now Let Us Rejoice

music by Henry Tucker
arranged by Brandon Eden

0:49

Organ

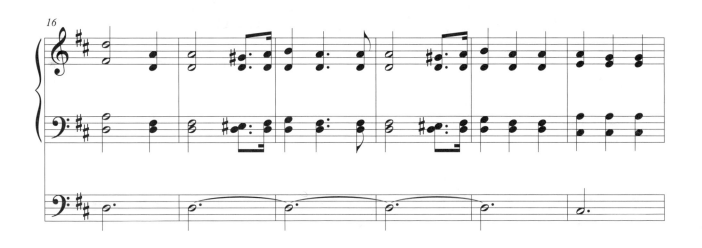

Now Let Us Rejoice Variation

music by Henry Tucker
arranged by Brandon Eden

0:49

O My Father

music by James McGranahan
arranged by Brandon Eden

0:55

O My Father Variation

music by James McGranahan
arranged by Brandon Eden

0:55

Praise to the Man

arranged by Brandon Eden

0:40

Organ

Praise to the Man Variation

arranged by Brandon Eden

0:40

Vigorously ♩ = 95

Organ

The Spirit of God

arranged by Brandon Eden

1:12

Exultantly ♩ = 110

Organ

35

The Spirit of God Variation

arranged by Brandon Eden

1:12

About the Author

Brandon Eden was born in New Mexico but grew up primarily in the Midwest. He began piano lessons at the age of five and composing at age ten. He competed in piano performances all through his teens and went to Brigham Young University, where he majored in music. While there, he specialized in keyboards, synthesis, and composition. He currently runs a small audio production studio and works at a music technology retailer.

SCAN to visit

WWW.BRANDONEDENMUSIC.COM